eco-anxiety

(and what to do about it)

Harriet Dyer

ECO-ANXIETY

Earth © A.Rom/Shutterstock.com; tree and hand illustrations © StocKNick/
Shutterstock.com; clouds © Retany/Shutterstock.com

Text by Claire Berrisford

Published in the United States by Viva Editions, an imprint of Start Midnight,
LLC, 221 River Street, Ninth Floor, Hoboken, New Jersey 07030

Trade Paper ISBN: 978-1-63228-084-8

E-book ISBN: 978-1-63228-141-8

DISCLAIMER
The author and the publisher cannot accept responsibility for any misuse or
misunderstanding of any information contained herein, or any loss, damage or
injury, be it health, financial or otherwise, suffered by any individual or group acting
upon or relying on information contained herein. None of the views or suggestions
in this book is intended to replace medical opinion from a doctor who is familiar
with your particular circumstances. If you have concerns about your health, please
seek professional advice.

contents

Introduction

Are you anxious about the future of the planet? Do you feel helpless when you think about climate change? Are you filled with the desire to *do something* to save the earth, but also overwhelmed when thinking about where to begin? If so, then you might be experiencing eco-anxiety.

For many people, eco-anxiety involves a complex mixture of feelings—including fear, frustration, grief, anxiety, helplessness and hopelessness—but, in a sentence, it can be summarized as a feeling of dread about the future of the environment. It's a reaction to what's going on in the world and, for many people, it's actually a healthy response, as it shows that you are empathizing with the plight of the natural world. However, eco-anxiety can be distressing and difficult to live with.

The first thing to know is that you are not alone. There are many people across the world who feel exactly the same way as you do. The second thing to know is that there are plenty of ways you can manage your feelings and live life with less environmental anxiety. You can care about the

earth without it being something overwhelming—
and that's where this book comes in.

Use the tips in the following pages in a way
that works for you. If you want advice about
feeling less distressed by what's going on, you
might find the first chapters helpful, as these
have tips on managing your fears, finding
calm and building up your resilience. If taking
action is what makes your eco-anxiety less
overwhelming, spend time looking at the later
chapters, which are all about living a more eco-
friendly life and getting involved in activism.

No matter how you're feeling—whether eco-
anxiety is an everyday worry or something that
occurs now and then—there will always be a
way to handle your feelings so you can be kind to
yourself as well as the planet.
Hopefully this book will
help you allay your
fears, as well
as provide you
with a dose of
calm, courage
and hope.

managing
eco-
anxiety

Eco-anxiety presents us with a whole bundle of challenging emotions, but one of the biggest to deal with is fear. Read the tips in this chapter to learn some ways to calm your fear and manage your anxiety about the environment.

You are not alone

Anxiety can be isolating. While you're feeling worried, it can seem like nobody knows or understands what you're going through and that everyone else is going about their lives unaffected. What's more, when your anxiety is related to the breakdown of our climate, it's likely to be triggered often—perhaps even multiple times a day—by headlines that forecast disaster. With the bad news piling up so quickly, it makes you feel helpless and even more isolated.

But you are not alone. In fact, there are millions of people around the world who care for the environment just like you do. The climate crisis is a worrying phenomenon, but it unites people around the world with a single aim: to save the planet. So, while eco-anxiety is scary and uncomfortable, remember that you are part of a global community, standing shoulder to shoulder with so many others who feel exactly the same as you do.

Share your concerns with others

If climate change is making you anxious—whether it's something that bothers you every now and again, or whether it's something you think about every day—the first step is to talk to a friend or someone you trust about how you're feeling. You could also phone a mental health helpline if you would prefer to speak anonymously. Opening up about how you feel can be incredibly challenging, but talking about what you're going through can make you feel better, and can help you to cope with the feelings you're dealing with. It also helps to share the burden and remind you that you are not facing your worries alone.

Don't let your thoughts spiral

It can be easy to let your thoughts run away with you. Constantly imagining the very worst possible scenario or outcome is something psychologists call "catastrophizing" and, if you experience eco-anxiety, you might be familiar with this feeling. One of the main symptoms of eco-anxiety is a sense of dread about the environment, so it doesn't help when the headlines we read focus on the worst-case scenario.

Making people aware of climate change and its potential consequences is important, but for those who are already worried, these headlines don't help. If you feel yourself beginning to catastrophize, take a moment. Approach your thought rationally; a bad result is possible, but it's not inevitable. Imagine a positive outcome, as this could happen too. Some people find saying "stop" out loud helps to halt catastrophic thinking in its tracks. Catastrophizing is also usually worse when you are stressed or tired, so if your thoughts are spiraling, take a break and try to unwind, as this will help you to feel calmer (for more ideas, see the tips in chapter two).

Worry window

We often put a lot of pressure on ourselves to *not* be worried, and this, in turn, can make feelings of anxiety worse, because we get anxious about the fact that we are feeling anxious. If this is a familiar feeling to you, you might want to try the following tip. Give yourself a small window every day—10 or 15 minutes—to worry as much as you want. The aim of this is not to psych yourself out or to try to reach a peak state of fear. It's simply time that you allow yourself to feel what you're feeling without any judgement. When the time is up, move on and do something else. If eco-anxiety threatens at any point in the day that's not in your window, write down your worry, and tell yourself that you will think about it later. It might seem counter-intuitive, but this technique allows you to acknowledge your feelings without being consumed by them.

Step back

It can feel like our duty to be informed about the world around us, especially with the causes we care about, such as the environment. When new studies and statistics appear every day, it's tempting to read up on them, whether it's because you want to know how serious the particular problem is, whether a headline is reliable, or what the news means for the future. However, if you're suffering from eco-anxiety, this might not be the best course of action. A lot of the time, it's unlikely that you will be able to do anything to solve the problem you're reading about, and knowing about it will only make you feel worse. It's okay not to read everything. It doesn't mean that you care about the cause any less, just because you didn't investigate this story, or post something about that video. It just means that you're putting your own mental health first.

Take a break

When an environmental disaster occurs, it can be hard to escape the wall-to-wall coverage that fills our social media and newsfeeds, whether you want to know more about it or not.

If you find yourself feeling distressed or anxious because of the intense coverage of an event, simply block it out. You could take a break from social media for a few days, or you could mute certain words and phrases on individual apps. Change the channel, turn down the radio, excuse yourself from a conversation—do whatever you need to do to put some distance between you and the event that has happened, and allow yourself some space to find calm.

One thing per day

When it comes to climate change, the important thing is not how much you do to help the cause, but the fact that you *are* doing something. If thinking about the environment leaves you feeling overwhelmed, take it slowly—try to just do one thing a day to improve your corner of the world. It doesn't have to be a big thing either. Your one act could be as simple as taking the time to recycle something instead of throwing it in the trash bin. You could buy the vegetables for your dinner at a local shop or market rather than a supermarket. You could mend an item of clothing instead of buying something new, or choose to drink your coffee in the shop rather than taking it away in a single-use cup.

Keep an "I did" list

When we're feeling disheartened, it's important to seek out positive things and hold onto them—and celebrate them! So, next time eco-anxiety hits and you feel like you're not making a difference, try keeping an "I did" list. This is simply a tally of every planet-friendly choice you've made. Write down all the things you've done today, or you could keep an "I did" diary for a week. Include everything on this list, even the tiny things like turning off the tap when you're brushing your teeth, or switching off a plug at the socket to save energy. Keeping a record in this way allows you to track your progress and see how you've made a difference. Look over your list as it grows, and think how much better off the world is because of your actions!

Little things add up

To change the story on climate change, the whole world needs to act. This thought is often at the heart of our eco-anxiety, because it's the thing that makes us feel most helpless. You might wonder whether there's any point in trying to help the earth: you're just one person, so how can you make an impact?

If these thoughts are familiar, then it's important to remember: change doesn't only happen on a large scale—it also happens in increments, with hundreds of tiny actions adding up to make a real difference. Take your "I did" list (see page 15) and imagine that multiplied by millions, because there are millions of people around the world making small changes every day to help the planet.

Perfectly imperfect

There are some pretty big lifestyle changes
you can choose to make if you want to help
the planet. For instance, you could follow a
plant-based diet, or you could pledge to go
zero-waste. If you're surrounded by people who
are making these drastic changes, you might
feel pressured into following suit: you might
feel that if you don't make these changes, your
efforts to save the planet are inadequate.

Despite what you might hear, a plant-based diet
or zero-waste living are not necessarily all-or-
nothing ventures. Reducing your meat and dairy
intake a little is better than not doing so at all;
buying fruit, veg and grains loose when you
can is better than always buying it wrapped in
plastic. The fact is, you don't have to follow a
vegan or a zero-waste lifestyle perfectly to make
a difference. Making little changes where you
can and how you can is what truly counts.

Be kind to yourself

If you're feeling anxious about the state of the world, the most important thing is to be kind to yourself. It's almost impossible to live a carbon-neutral life, so don't be hard on yourself or feel ashamed if you have to make a less eco-friendly choice. Maybe you have to fly somewhere, or perhaps the product you need only comes wrapped in plastic. Maybe the eco-friendly choice is too expensive or time-consuming, or it just might not be practical for the situation you're in right now. If so, then don't worry: as long as you're doing your best then that's all anybody can ask for.

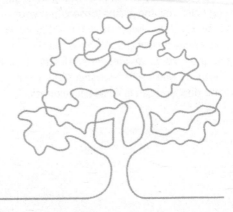

finding
calm

Another one of eco-anxiety's most notable symptoms is the one in its name: anxiety. Before we can even think about helping the planet, we have to be able to help ourselves. This chapter is full of tips on how to calm your anxiety in the moment and manage your feelings, so that you can move onward, thinking clearly and feeling calmer.

Ground yourself

Feeling anxious often means we are stuck in our heads, plagued with racing thoughts, or unable to shake off our worry about the future. If you experience these feelings, try this short exercise to bring yourself back to the present moment. First, pay attention to your breathing, making sure it is slow and deep. Then gently turn your attention to your surroundings. What tiny details can you see? Can you notice anything you haven't seen before? Widen your attention to your other senses. What can you hear, feel or smell? Tell yourself that you are in the here and now. Focusing intently on the tangible aspects of your immediate moment can help to stop feelings of anxiety in their tracks and allow you to regroup.

Meditation

Meditation is the art of allowing your mind to become completely still, like a pool of water with no ripples, and it's a good way to calm feelings of anxiety. To begin, find a quiet, uncluttered place and sit in a comfortable position. Close your eyes if you like. Take slow, steady breaths and focus your attention on them. If a thought comes into your mind, acknowledge it but don't pursue it. Remain focused on your breathing. Notice if any parts of your body feel tense—if so, relax them. Let yourself be still and soft. Do this for as long as you would like to, whether that's for five minutes or for half an hour. Bear in mind that meditation is a skill that comes with practice, so keep at it even if it's hard at first. There are also plenty of guided meditation apps that you can try if you want more support.

Get out into nature

When you're anxious, making sure that you have enough fresh air is one of the best things you can do to help yourself to feel better. If you can, spend time in a green space, as being around plants and trees has been proven to lower stress levels, and feeling the grass under your feet is a great way to reconnect to nature. Walk through a park, garden, field or forest, and notice the sounds and atmosphere around you, or simply sit quietly and feel the sun and the breeze on your face. Even if there aren't green spaces near you, a walk outside can still boost your mood. As long as the sky and the clouds are above you, nature can help to make you feel more at ease.

Good food, good mood

It may seem unrelated, but your diet is an important factor in helping you feel calm, and eating the right things can have a hugely positive effect on your mood. Eating three meals a day at regularly spaced intervals will maintain your blood sugar levels and keep you from feeling hungry and irritable. Eating at least five portions of fruit and vegetables a day is important too, as these will give you the right vitamins to help your brain function at its best. If stress is making you crave a snack, rather than reaching for something fatty or sugary, try foods such as carrots, vegetable chips, berries, bananas, apples, whole grain crackers, plain popcorn, black olives or almonds, as these will give you the crunch/sweetness/saltiness you are craving without the empty calories. You don't have to overhaul your whole lifestyle at once, but making small, healthy choices every day can go a long way to making you feel calmer and happier.

Get moving

Exercise is not only good for your body—it's good for your mind too! Getting out and moving your body releases serotonin, which is both a mood booster and a stress buster. Even something as simple as walking is beneficial and easy to incorporate into your day. Try walking to work or taking a 20-minute stroll in your lunch break, for instance. You could do some jumping jacks or squats while you wait for the kettle to boil, do some exercises while you watch TV, or run up and down the stairs a couple of times to raise your heart rate. However you choose to move, being more active will help you to relax, sleep better and feel more positive, all of which will ultimately help you feel calmer.

4-7-8 breathing

Here is a simple breathing exercise you can try at any point during your day to soothe any anxious feelings.

Find a place where you can sit or lie comfortably. Place the tip of your tongue against the tissue just above your front teeth. Keep it there throughout the exercise. Empty your lungs completely. Breathe in quietly through your nose for four seconds. Hold the breath for seven seconds. Exhale through your mouth for eight seconds, allowing the breath to make a slight "whoosh" sound through your lips as you do. Repeat this cycle another three times.

If you feel light-headed after trying this for the first time, sit down and wait for the feeling to pass. If you can't hold your breath for the full seven seconds, try shorter intervals at first: breathe in for two seconds, hold for three seconds, and breathe out for four.

Write it out

However anxiety affects your thoughts—whether it makes them race, or whether it makes them fixate on particular things—putting pen to paper can be a good way to soothe your mind. Many people find that writing out their feelings can be therapeutic, as it helps to put a little distance between them and their thoughts. Sometimes, simply the act of putting your feelings into words and defining them calms you, as it helps you to understand your emotions rather than letting them hover in your mind. It doesn't matter whether you write physically in a journal or type your feelings onto your phone or your computer. However you choose to do it, it's the act of truly acknowledging your thoughts that helps you to find peace of mind.

Get enough sleep

Did you know that sleep is as important as diet and exercise in keeping us healthy? It also has a big part to play in keeping our mood balanced and positive, so if you're feeling anxious, getting enough sleep is a good step to feeling better. The average person functions best with eight hours' sleep a night, although some people may need slightly more or less.

If you find it difficult to drop off, here are a few tips you could try:

Bedtime routine: Have a routine that you follow at the same time every night before you go to bed. Perhaps you could read a chapter of a book, do some yoga or ten minutes of meditation before settling down, or you could prepare your clothes and a to-do list for the following day. Whatever routine you choose, make sure you stick to it, as, after a while, this will help to signal to your body that it's time to sleep.

Consistency: Try to get up at roughly the same time each day—even at the weekend—as this helps to maintain your sleep pattern.

Screens away: Try to avoid looking at screens for at least 30 minutes before you go to sleep. The bright light from a screen makes your brain more alert, so to give yourself the best chance of winding down, leave your phones and tablets alone before bedtime.

A hot bath: Your body cools down as you fall asleep; having a hot bath warms you up—which then triggers your body into cooling you down, and easing you into sleep.

Pillow spray: Some people find using a pillow spray helps to ease them into sleep. They are usually infused with scents such as lavender or chamomile, which help to promote sleep.

Temperature: The optimum room temperature to promote good sleep is between 16 and 18°C (60–64°F).

Ear plugs: If you are a light sleeper, use earplugs to muffle the noise around you.

Darkness: A dark room helps to signal to your brain that it's time to sleep, so turn off any lights or electrical items and use heavy curtains. Alternatively, try using an eye mask.

Self-care

Self-care is anything that you do to help to protect or nurture your own health and well-being, and when you're feeling anxious, it's especially important. An act of self-care could be a mundane everyday task, or it could be an indulgent treat—it is anything that contributes to your sense of wellness and keeps you feeling happy and healthy.

If you don't know where to start with self-care, think about what makes you happy and satisfied. Perhaps self-care for you could mean cooking yourself a delicious meal, phoning a friend, watching a film or going for a run. Pursuing a hobby is another effective act of self-care, as you're doing something just for the joy of it.

Self-care can be small too. It can be as simple as taking five minutes in the morning to have a leisurely cup of coffee, listen to birdsong or go for a walk around the block. It can be hugging a loved one or stroking a pet, cloud-watching, lighting a candle or listening to your favorite artist. Even the tiniest moments can be restorative.

Self-care doesn't just mean treating yourself to the things that make you happy, either. It also means keeping up the little chores of day-to-day life, like brushing your teeth, doing the laundry and washing the dishes. They may seem insignificant or boring, but these small actions are a hugely valuable part of looking after yourself, and keeping up with them makes you feel calmer and more in control.

Don't be afraid to cry

It's often our gut reaction to hold our tears back, but crying is a healthy and perfectly natural process. As well as being a way to release stress and tension, it means that you're acknowledging and confronting your feelings instead of bottling them up and pushing them away, which is always a healthier way to deal with them. Tears aren't just a way of expressing your emotions either—they also have health benefits, as they help to cleanse the body of the chemicals that raise cortisol, the stress hormone. So, if you're particularly anxious and you feel the urge to cry, that's your body's way of trying to make you feel better. Shutting the door and letting it all out will release your tension and help you feel ready to face the world again.

Seek help

If your anxiety is getting in the way of everyday life, speak to your doctor, as they will be able to offer you professional advice on how to manage your feelings. They may recommend therapy, medication or relaxation techniques to help with your situation—however you proceed, a doctor will be able to talk you through your options and help you find the best path for you.

Deciding to seek outside help and opening up to someone else can be challenging, but, if you're finding it difficult to cope with your feelings, it's one of the best things you can do to help yourself move forward.

building

resilience

According to the American Psychological Association, the vital skills that help us to cope with the thought of climate change are mental resilience and optimism. These might sound hard to attain, but this chapter has you covered, showing you ways to deal with adversity and bounce back when things don't go to plan, as well as giving you tips on how to foster a more positive outlook. By spending time developing this kind of mindset, you will be better equipped to deal with the feelings of eco-anxiety.

Choose your response to situations

When something "bad" happens, we usually have a choice: we can choose to react negatively, or we can remain calm and look for a solution. Our knee-jerk reactions are often habits we've fallen into, so it's important to realize we always have a choice—that we can respond to a situation rather than react to it. When you're faced with a setback, a disappointment or a piece of negative news, pause for a moment and consciously decide how you would like to respond. Taking this time to consider gives us the opportunity to act more rationally in a situation rather than letting our immediate emotions take over, and this means we can move forward more calmly, feeling like we are in control.

Believe in yourself

It may sound corny, but it's true: you have to believe in yourself. To improve your resilience, believe in your own ability to overcome stress— because you can! Our mental attitude is largely down to the stories we tell ourselves about our situation and our abilities. Simply by believing that you have the inner strength and power to get through your current situation, you help yourself to feel more confident. It can be tricky, but once you allow yourself to have a little faith in your own abilities, this will pave the way for even more resilience and the ability to think positively.

Failure is not permanent

Setbacks are an inevitable part of life, but the key to a resilient mindset is not to view them as permanent. You may be disappointed at something that's happened, or perhaps you have failed at something. It's okay to be downhearted during these times, but try to see them as a chapter of a book rather than the whole story. Even though you may be in the midst of a negative experience right now, that doesn't mean that things won't change for the better.

Change your ABC

Many of us believe that negative events cause us to behave in a certain way, but research reveals that our reactions are based on our individual thoughts about adversity. This explains why people respond differently to the same stressful situation.

A person might experience adversity (A), such as being disheartened and anxious about the state of the environment. They might then have the belief (B) that they are helpless and that nothing can be done. As a consequence (C), they would sink into despair and not be motivated to help the earth. Another person in the same situation might recognize that there are many problems in the world, but they'd take this as an opportunity to do something about it. They may feel sad or worried about the world, but they would be optimistic about the future and decide to take action to try to make a difference. Reflecting carefully on the ABCs in your life may help you change your mindset and make it easier to overcome difficulties rather than letting them overwhelm you.

Rethink stress

Reframing negative emotions and taking them away from the associations that we give them can help us to be more resilient. For instance, begin to see stress as a professional athlete views his or her workout—as an opportunity to grow stronger. Stress builds character. It isn't necessarily comfortable, but it tests your resolve and problem-solving abilities. Look at it as a workout for your mind.

You could even deliberately set a challenge for yourself: how calmly can you steer through life, despite the bumps in the road? Viewing stress in a more positive light can help you embrace the challenges and obstacles that you encounter.

You are the main character

Allowing ourselves to be the main character in the story of our own lives helps us to build up our resilience. It's easy to see each passing day as something that just "happens" to us, especially if we're dealing with a string of negative experiences. Instead, try thinking of life as a narrative that you're physically taking part in. You are making choices for yourself, taking your experiences of life so far and deciding how to act because of them. When we have this sense of agency, it helps us to feel more in control.

Reframe failure

Reframing how we see failure can help us to be mentally stronger. When things don't go to plan, we often experience "failure" the moment we realize our expectations are not going to be met. We get caught up in the feelings that come with it, like anger, embarrassment, disappointment or sadness. To build up your resilience, try to redefine what "failure" is. Remember that we never truly fail until we stop trying—it's when we don't get back up after a fall that we have accepted defeat. So, even when things feel bleak, try your best to pick yourself up and carry on or try again, because if you stand back up, you haven't failed.

Have a purpose

Inner strength often comes from how we create
meaning in our lives. In other words, we need
a purpose: an anchor that keeps us steady and
grounded, and prevents us from floating freely and
feeling lost. If you don't know what your purpose
is, think about what you love and enjoy, and what
makes you want to get out of bed in the morning.
Have something or someone, a community, a
cause or a hobby that you care about, as it's
this that will connect you to your life and inspire
you to keep going when times are tough.

Foster optimism

People will often say that pessimism is a realistic mindset to be in: if you expect the worst, you'll be prepared when it happens, or pleasantly surprised when things go better than you expected.

However, it's not necessarily as simple as this. Having a pessimistic or optimistic outlook can significantly change the way you experience life. A pessimist tends to approach life expecting to see problems, seeing setbacks as innate and unchangeable. In contrast, an optimist will approach problems with a mindset that's ready to look for a solution. Optimism is also linked with longer life expectancy, greater happiness, improved recovery from illness and, most importantly here, a greater ability to recover from setbacks and cope with negative experiences.

It's not always easy; to be optimistic, you have to allow yourself to hang on to a little bit of hope for the future, even if things aren't looking positive in that moment. This makes optimism more difficult because it means opening yourself up to the possibility of disappointment. However, by allowing yourself to be vulnerable in this way, you make yourself stronger. It's having faith in our ability to cope, and in the fact that things can get better, that helps to pull us through difficult times.

Pessimism may be easier, but optimism will help you to live a longer, happier and more resilient life. The tips in the rest of this chapter all focus on ways that you can continue to develop this habit of positive thinking.

Challenge your thoughts

A positive mindset begins with our thoughts, as these are the lens through which we see the world. If you're about to try something new and you're thinking "This is going to go badly", "I will be terrible at this" or "I don't want to be here", then the chances are that you won't have a good time.

Take notice of the language of your thoughts and, next time you catch a negative one, try reframing it. For instance, "This is too hard" or "I can't do this" could become "This is hard but I will try my best." Thoughts such as "I am helpless" or "There is nothing I can do" could become, "I feel helpless, but I know that even small actions can make a difference" or "I will do whatever I can do."

Focus on your strengths

If you're coping with a setback, or you're struggling with some bad news, a good way to metaphorically dust yourself off and stand back up again is to focus on your strengths. Tell yourself all the things that you're good at in your head or, even better, write them down so that you can see the list growing in front of you. If you're downhearted by your situation, go to your list of strengths and let it give you a boost. Focusing on what you *can* do is a great way to bolster your confidence at the times when you need it most.

Affirmations

An affirmation is a short phrase that you can say to help to center yourself. They can be used for all manner of situations: to help you to control anger, to motivate you, to boost your self-confidence or, as in the examples here, to help inspire a positive mindset.

When you need a boost, you can write your affirmation down, recite it to yourself or, best of all, say it out loud while looking in the mirror. Look yourself in the eye, hold your head up, release the tension from your shoulders and say your affirmation to your reflection with as much confidence and assurance as you can.

The key to affirmations is focusing on the positive outcome that you want rather than the negative possibility that you wish to avoid. Write your own, specific to your circumstances, or try any of the following phrases to set an intention for your day:

I am calm and I am happy

I will have a good day

I inhale positivity and exhale negativity

I have everything I need

I am brimming with energy

I am good enough

I am right where I need to be

I am ready for whatever the day brings

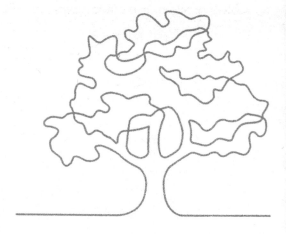

Practice gratitude

Gratitude is a simple thing, but it can have a big effect on your outlook and your mood. Try to find at least three things to be grateful for each day, no matter how small they are. Perhaps the sun shone today, or perhaps you had a great cup of coffee. These are all small moments that can make a difference to our whole day if we notice them and celebrate them. Why not keep a journal of the things you're grateful for? This is an effective way to help you focus on the positive aspects of the day and gets you into the habit of finding joy in the little things.

Surround yourself with sunshine

It's hard to be positive if the people around you are bringing you down. Pay attention to your mood as you go about your day. Do your colleagues make you feel happy or drained? How do you feel after you get home from socializing with your friends? Is there a particular place or person that affects your mood? If you do notice that a person or group of people is making you feel negative, consider distancing yourself from them for a bit and see how you feel. Everybody deserves to be around people who lift them up and support them, so if the people around you are not doing this then don't be afraid to try making changes.

Let your body talk

It might feel like your mind and body are two separate entities, but one can affect the other. You can use the connection between the two to help develop a more positive outlook. First, try to avoid slouching. Instead, keep your back straight and your shoulders relaxed and open—this works whether you're standing up or sitting down. Presenting yourself as open and relaxed will help you to feel the same way. A bonus is that this position makes it easier to breathe fully and deeply, which will also help to improve your mood.

If you're walking anywhere, take control of your posture. Our habit is often to look at the ground, so instead, keep your head up, stand tall and walk at a swift pace. Imagine you're a superhero walking down the street with all the confidence in the world.

Another way to trick your body into feeling happier is simply to smile, even if you're not feeling like it. When you smile, the movement of your muscles triggers the release of endorphins, which makes us happier. It also helps to reduce levels of the stress hormone cortisol. Your brain can't tell the difference between a real and a fake smile, so even if you're not feeling it inside, give smiling a go.

Being aware of your body language in this way often feels strange at the beginning, and you might feel self-conscious about "pretending" to be relaxed and happy, but if you keep it up, pretty soon you won't be pretending any more.

supporting
others

When the people around you are feeling down or anxious about the environment, it can be hard to know what to do or say to make them feel better, or even how to talk about the topic. This chapter covers a few tips to help you support friends, family and the people around you who are experiencing eco-anxiety.

Validation

If someone around you expresses that they're worried or scared about the state of the environment, try to validate rather than minimize their emotions. Our instinct is often to try to reassure the other person by telling them "I'm sure it will all be fine" or "Don't worry, things will work out." Although these kinds of responses can be soothing, they're not always useful because they effectively ignore feelings of anxiety, which, in the long run, will probably make them feel worse. Instead, acknowledge the other person's feelings and concentrate on positive actions or news stories. Remind them that it's okay to be worried, but that they should try to focus on moving forward.

Find answers together

Don't feel that you have to be an expert to be able to support the people around you. We want to reassure friends, family and children by providing them with answers—especially for young children, who are still full of questions about the world—but climate change is a vast topic and it's impossible to know everything. It's completely okay not to know the answer to something straight away. Use these times as a chance to look things up together. Not only will this help you to get more accurate information—rather than providing a vague answer—but it will help everyone involved to feel that they are not alone in their worries.

Reconnect with nature

Sometimes, simply spending time in the great
outdoors can be a tonic for our worries, especially
when they are focused on the environment. If you
have a friend or family member who is anxious,
take a trip together and spend time in a park or
garden, go to the sea or down to a river, climb a
hill or walk through a forest. Reconnect with the
natural world by immersing yourself in it. Take time
to notice all the things around you: what can you
each see, hear and smell, and how many plants
can you name? You could even search together
for a small memento—a rock or pebble to keep in
your pocket to ground you when you feel anxious,
or a flower or leaf to press and keep in a spot
that you'll see to help inspire you and remind
you of your connection to the natural world.

Stick to the facts

There is nothing wrong with being worried about the climate crisis; it's a legitimate cause for concern, and the fact that a person is worried shows that they have empathy and that they care about what is happening. However, in a world where fake news and scaremongering headlines are all too common, it's important not to get caught up in hearsay and rumors, which can make anxiety worse. To look after our well-being, we need to make sure we stick to the facts. This is particularly important when it comes to supporting younger children through eco-anxiety. If a child expresses that they're worried or scared, talk to them about what they think is happening, and make sure, together, that you have a realistic picture of what is going on that's grounded in facts.

Talk about social media

If you have a friend or family member who is experiencing eco-anxiety, talk to them about how much they use social media or how often they watch or listen to the news. Scrolling through a newsfeed or homepage where everyone is talking about the issue of the moment, or hearing bulletins repeatedly, only serve to amplify feelings of anxiety and put the issue at the forefront of their mind, so encourage your friend or family member to take a step back. If you are caring for a child or young person, make sure you are aware of how much they are exposed to news stories about the environment, and consider monitoring their use of social media to help protect their mental well-being.

Start the conversation

We can often tell when our close friends and family are worried about something, but they don't always want to talk, whether it's because they don't know where to start, or because they're reluctant to feel vulnerable. Instead of waiting for them to say something, initiate a conversation yourself and create the space for them to discuss their feelings.

Even if your friends aren't showing signs of being worried, take care to check in with them anyway, because you never know who might want to get something off their chest. It's hard to open up to other people about how we're feeling, even to close friends, so offering the conversation might be the lifeline that they need.

If you want to initiate a discussion with a younger child, try providing opportunities for conversation about the environment. For instance, as you're unpacking the shopping, explain why you're using a tote bag instead of a plastic one, or talk to them about why you're picking up litter that you see while you're out and about.

Find success stories

The negative things we hear always stick in our mind more than the positives. We'll all have experienced this in relation to compliments and criticisms, or reviews of our work and performance. The same goes for news stories: negative stories about the environment have much more of an impact than positive ones, and they have the power to change our perception of the world. However, although the news is often negative, it's not all bad all the time. Keep your eye out for positive stories, and when you find one, save it, bookmark it—do whatever you need to do so that you can go back and find it in the future. The next time you're having a conversation with a friend about the environment, refer to the pockets of positivity that you've found and focus on these instead of the negatives.

Take action together

If the people around you are experiencing eco-anxiety, resolve to take action together. You and a friend could spend a weekend making some eco-friendly beauty products together, or you could lift-share with a colleague instead of both driving, or walk to work together. If you are supporting younger children, try to keep your efforts tangible and local. For instance, you could take part in a beach clean or go litter picking in the community, or you could sort the recycling together. Staying connected to the people around you is one of the best ways to help support both yourself and others through eco-anxiety, plus it's good for the planet.

Goal-getters

Choose an eco-goal with a friend, with colleagues, or as a family, and work together to make it happen. Perhaps you could aim to have one trash bag of garbageper week instead of two, eat meat only once a week, or aim to go plastic-free for a few days. The doomed feeling of eco-anxiety is largely to do with the fact that it seems like we receive a constant stream of bad news, and very little in the way of positives, so having a tangible, achievable goal is a good way to beat it. Even if you don't quite reach your goal—perhaps there was some plastic packaging that you weren't able to avoid—remember that it doesn't negate all the other times you were able to make the eco-friendly choice.

eco-living
tips

One of the best ways to manage eco-anxiety is to be proactive and do something about the environment! Reducing your carbon footprint is all about using less plastic, producing less waste and making better choices for the earth. But where do you start? There are so many ways that you can make good choices for the earth for every budget and situation. This chapter will tell you everything you need to know to get going.

Eat less meat

One of the biggest positive choices you can make toward helping the planet is to eat less meat. The meat itself is not the biggest issue—it's all the energy that goes into producing it that has an impact on the planet. The process of rearing, keeping and transporting farm animals takes around 11 times more fossil fuels and six times more water than plant-based foods, which is why cutting down on your meat consumption is a good way to minimize your carbon footprint. Here are a few tips on how to eat less meat and more plants:

- Don't pressure yourself to make changes too fast. If you eat meat every day, start slowly and try to have one meat-free day per week. If you have meat three times a week, try having it only once or twice a week. The key to making a lasting change is to go gradually.

- Explore vegetarian meat substitutes: vegetarian mince, fake meat, seitan or tofu.

- Find vegetarian alternatives for your favorite meaty dishes—think Bolognese made with vegetarian mince; portobello mushroom or cauliflower steaks; pulled pork made from jackfruit; bean burgers; or curries with aubergine instead of meat.

- Take the pressure off by planning your meals ahead of time. It makes meals one less thing to think about every day.

- Don't eat meat just for the sake of it—if you have a pasta bake or stir fry and always throw in chicken or bacon out of habit, try substituting an extra vegetable for the meat. You will barely notice the difference.

- Eat plenty of beans. Not only are they an excellent and varied way to consume the nutrients that you'd usually get from meat, they are low in fat, planet-friendly and a good substitute for meat in themselves.

- Add cereal and grains, such as couscous, quinoa, rice or barley to your meals and salads. They are high in protein, so help to make up the nutritional value from cutting out meat.

If you're hungry, snack on nuts, which are rich in protein and healthy fats. Walnuts, pistachios and hazelnuts are all excellent options, and you only need a small handful to fill you up for hours.

Have fun and be inspired: explore vegetarian cookbooks for more ideas. If you're used to meat featuring as the main part of your meal, this is a particularly good way to change your perspective and see that vegetables can also be the star of the show!

Shop seasonally and locally

When we shop from local producers and eat what's in season, we are reducing our carbon footprint. This is because there are fewer processes between the food growing and the point at which we buy it. And it's not only good for the earth. Buying seasonally and locally is usually cheaper (as the food has not had to be imported), supports local farms and businesses, and the produce is often tastier and more nutritious (because it spends less time in transit and the nutrients have less time to break down). Here are some tips on how to shop locally:

- Most food has its origin either printed on the packaging or indicated on the label on the shelf. Generally, the closer the origin of the food, the less distance it has had to travel to get to you, and the smaller its carbon footprint.

- Look out for local markets where farmers can sell their produce directly to you.

- Shop at local food stores and bakeries when you can.

Reduce food packaging

Even if you do try to buy food with a small carbon footprint, another problem we often face that undoes our good work is food packaging. Food items are commonly wrapped in plastic or have extra layers of packaging that will end up going straight in the trash bin. Here are a few ways you can reduce the amount of food packaging that you use.

- If you're in a supermarket or a larger local shop, opt for loose fruit and vegetables when you can. If you don't want them loose in your cart, you can put them in reusable mesh bags that are available to buy at most supermarkets.

- Buy meat at a butcher's and ask for your purchases to be put in a reusable container. It will probably be easiest for you to bring one (or several) with you.

- Explore getting fruit, vegetables and milk delivered to you, as these options often involve cardboard or glass packaging that's easier to recycle.

- Bring a fold-away, reusable bag with you every time you go shopping to avoid accepting plastic ones.

How to reduce your food waste

Millions of tons of food is wasted every year. Not only does it contribute to landfill sites, but it means that huge amounts of energy is wasted in growing, preparing and shipping food that's just going to go in the trash bin. However, there are simple ways you can reduce your household's amount of food waste. Take a look at the tips below.

- Plan your meals before you go food shopping so you only buy as much as you need.

- Try planning your meals around the food you already have. For instance, you might have half a jar of sauce, some spare vegetables, or half a bag of salad lying around; instead of letting these items spoil, find a recipe that allows you to use them up.

- Use leftovers as your lunch for the following day. If there's only a small portion left, try having it on some toast.

- If you've bought ingredients for specific recipes in your food shop, plan the order of your meals according to the use-by dates on the food.

Batch-cook meals: this means cooking a large amount in one go, serving what you need and then freezing or storing the rest for a different day (if you do this, add the date you made it to the container so you can keep track of when you should use it up).

If you find that your bread goes stale before the end of the loaf, buy sliced bread and keep it in the freezer. You can defrost slices as and when you need them, or toast bread from frozen.

Vegetables that are past their prime are fantastic in soups, pies or stews.

Turn old fruit into jams, compotes, chutneys and pickles. Not only are they delicious and a great way to jazz up your meals, but they will keep for months.

Keep apples and pears fresh by wrapping them in newspaper and storing them in a cool place. They can last up to three or four months this way.

Store onions and potatoes separately from each other, and ideally in a cool, dark, ventilated place. Both these foods release moisture, which means that they spoil more quickly when they are kept together.

Recycle

We all know that recycling is one simple way to help the planet. While you are probably already in the habit of putting paper, plastic, cardboard and glass in the recycling bin, here are some tips to help you take it to the next level and recycle like a pro:

 Always check for specific instructions about how to recycle packaging, and don't assume that the whole thing is recyclable.

 Compact your recycling as much as possible before you put it in the trash bin—crush cans, deconstruct cardboard boxes and squash the air out of plastic bottles. This gives you more space!

 Rinse and dry items before putting them in the recycling, as food left on containers can sometimes render entire batches of recycling completely unusable.

 Ensure that your recycling is dry before it goes in the recycling bin—particularly cardboard, which can clog up the sorting machines if wet.

Not all areas will recycle the same things. If there is a particular material that can't be recycled near you, look up the nearest facility online.

Have a small recycling bin in every room—or in the places where you often find yourself disposing of scraps of paper or plastic. This makes recycling more convenient, and therefore more likely to happen!

Don't forget that electrical appliances such as toasters, microwaves, televisions, DVDs, hairdryers and fridges can be recycled too at designated places.

Old batteries and soft plastics (such as bread bags, carrier bags or chip packets) aren't usually accepted in home recycling bins so, instead, save them up and take them to your local recycling point—often at a supermarket—where these items can be sorted and passed on to specialist recycling plants.

Know your plastics

There are many different kinds of plastic used in packaging. Some are easily recyclable, and some are not. Here is a quick guide to help you out:

- **PET or PETE (polyethylene terephthalate):** mainly used for clear drinks bottles and some food packaging. It's recyclable but shouldn't be reused, as repeated use can lead to a build-up of bacteria.

- **HDPE (high-density polyethylene):** mainly used as bottles for items such as milk, liquid soap and cosmetics. This plastic is both recyclable and reusable.

- **PVC (polyvinyl chloride):** used for clear food wrapping, shower curtains and toys. This is difficult to recycle.

- **LDPE (low-density polyethylene):** generally used for carrier bags, squeezable bottles and four-/six-pack can holders. It's currently difficult to recycle, although plans are in place to try to change this. A number of supermarkets take carrier bags for recycling.

PP (polypropylene): used for cereal bags, bottle tops, margarine tubs, snack bags (for things like potato chips) and straws. It is reusable and occasionally recyclable.

PS (polystyrene): you'll probably often see this as packaging for fragile objects and takeout cups. It's not reusable and it's also difficult to recycle. However, plans are in place to try to change this.

This list isn't exhaustive. There are many other types of plastic, such as acrylic glass, nylon, polycarbonate and items made of a mixture of plastics. These are not reusable and they are also difficult to recycle.

Reuse

Recycling is good for the earth, but reusing is even better. Here are some creative ways to get the most out of everyday objects you might ordinarily recycle or throw away:

- Some items that we tend to think of as single-use can be used multiple times: kitchen foil can be reused, sandwich bags can be washed and margarine tubs can be used as containers for the freezer.

- Use plastic carrier bags more than once. Why not fold one small and keep it in your bag so you always have one to hand? If they're not strong, you could use them as trash bin liners.

- Use torn plastic bags for crafting—there are plenty of ideas online, from weaving them into baskets to making them into jewelery, art pieces or even rugs.

- Donate unwanted clothes to charity to prevent them from ending up in landfill, or give them away to family and friends.

- Use tin cans as planters for window-ledge herbs, as a desk tidy to keep pens and pencils in, or puncture a pattern into the sides and put a tea light inside to make a tiny lantern.

- Use rechargeable batteries instead of single-use ones. They are slightly more expensive to buy in the first instance, but they can be recharged between 500 and 1,000 times, so they will make their money back many times over in the long run.

- A used teabag can be turned into a trash bin freshener: wait until it's dry, add a few drops of essential oil and place at the bottom of the trash bin.

- Yesterday's newspapers can also be used to shine mirrors and clean windows. Add a splash of household vinegar to a scrunched-up sheet and rub the glazed area until it gleams.

- Old toothbrushes can be demoted to household cleaning duty and be used to clean delicate or intricate items.

- A mesh fruit/vegetable bag can be scrunched up and used as a scrubber in the kitchen.

Save energy

There are tons of easy ways to save energy in everyday life, and it's the small changes that add up to make a big difference. Here are some simple tips:

Use a smart meter or an app on your phone to monitor how much energy you're using. This will help you to understand your own energy usage, and tell you when you're using lots in one go.

- Turn off the lights when you leave a room. Before you know it, it'll be a habit!

- Use eco-friendly bulbs in your light fittings.

- Turn off plug switches at the socket when you're not using them, as there can be energy flowing through an appliance even when it's on standby.

- Turn the thermostat down, as central heating is a big energy user in the home. When it gets cold, put an extra layer on or snuggle up under a blanket instead of immediately turning up the heat.

- Use draft excluders to keep your home toasty and warm. You can invest in these or simply make your own by stuffing an old pair of tights with newspaper.

- Insulate your home a little more by keeping the curtains closed. This way, less heat is able to escape through the glass of your windows.

- When you're cooking, keep a lid on your pans so that the food heats up more quickly.

- Only boil what you need in the kettle to avoid heating up water that you're not going to use.

- Opt for a cool cycle on your washing machine, and dry your laundry outside rather than in a tumble dryer.

- Consider getting cavity wall insulation in your home. You may be able to apply for a government grant to get money off this service.

Conserve water

Here are some top tips on simple ways to save water around the home:

- Use a water-saving device in your toilet cistern. These devices usually work by taking up space in the cistern, meaning that there's less room for the water and therefore less water used per flush.

- Don't flush the toilet every time you use it – "If it's yellow, let it mellow."

- Turn off the taps when you're not using them, for instance, when you brush your teeth or wash your face.

- Take quick showers instead of baths. Alternatively, take shallow baths instead of long showers.

- While you're in the shower, turn off the water while you're shampooing your hair to save a few extra liters.

- Wear clothes more than once rather than putting them in the laundry basket after every use. Only wash them when they really need cleaning.

Collect waste water and use it for other things. For instance, if you're washing your hands or rinsing vegetables in the kitchen, collect the water and use it in the garden or to water your houseplants.

Reuse pans of water for cooking—some recipes call for a fresh pan of water, but in many cases you could easily reuse it.

When you're washing the dishes, use a bowl of washing-up water rather than washing everything under running water.

Fix any dripping taps as soon as you can. A drip may seem small but the water it wastes adds up quickly!

Only run the dishwasher when it's full. Don't forget that you can often put other kitchen items in the dishwasher to fill it up, such as mixing bowls, pots and pans.

If you water your garden regularly, do it at cooler times of day as less water will evaporate.

Use a bucket of water and a sponge to clean the car rather than running a hose continuously.

Cleaning tips

We often use a lot of chemicals to clean our homes, but they can be harmful to the environment. Here are some recipes for cleaning products that are natural and chemical-free.

Liquid soap

Mix 3 tbsp liquid Castile soap, 250 ml (0.4 pt) warm water, 2 tbsp white vinegar and a few drops of pine or lavender essential oil in a screw-cap or squeezy bottle. Close the lid firmly and give it a good shake to mix well. When you want to wash up, squirt about a two teaspoons of the mixture into warm water and swirl with your hands. It won't be as bubbly as store-bought liquid soap, but it works just as well. (Note: be mindful of allergies if you choose not to wear cleaning gloves.)

Toilet cleaner

Mix 100 g (3.5 oz) bicarbonate of soda with a few drops of tea tree oil and a few drops of pine essential oil in a clean, empty jam jar. When it's time to clean the toilet, pour 250 ml (0.4 pt) white vinegar into the bicarbonate of soda mixture. When the mixture is fizzing, pour it into and around the toilet bowl and leave it to work its magic. Flush away when the mixture has stopped fizzing.

Disinfectant

Mix 250 ml (0.4 pt) white vinegar, 1 tbsp bicarbonate of soda and 1 liter (1.75 pt) hot water in a large bowl or bucket. Squeeze the juice of half a lemon or lime into the water and mix. Decant the mixture into a spray bottle and use it in the same way as any other all-purpose cleaner.

Laundry detergent

Take one bar of soap and grate it, either in a food processor or by hand. Put the grated soap in a large bowl and add 500 g (17.5 oz) soda crystals. Mix well, transfer to an airtight container, and use in the same way you'd use any other detergent.

Fabric softener

Mix 500 ml (0.9 pt) white vinegar with 25 drops of essential oil (lemon or lavender work well). Transfer mixture to a 500-ml jam jar or bottle and use the same way you'd use any other fabric softener. (Always shake well before use.)

Reduce paper use

Paper is widely recyclable, so it's definitely not the most problematic of all our household materials. However, it still requires a lot of water to produce, so minimizing the amount of paper we use is another step toward reducing our carbon footprint. Here are some tips:

- If you subscribe to any magazines or newspapers, switch to a digital version.

- Unsubscribe from companies who send you catalogs or junk mail.

- Go paperless with your bank and view your statements online.

- Read e-books as much as you can, buy books second-hand or swap books with friends so that you're not accumulating too much extra paper.

- Opt for e-tickets wherever you can—for flights, train journeys or events.

Where possible, ask for digital versions—work documents, receipts, spreadsheets and other paperwork (even contracts and legal documents) can nearly all be viewed just as well on screen rather than as a printed-out version and can be stored forever!

Try not to print things unless you absolutely have to.

Sometimes we can't escape the need to use paper. In these situations, try to use recycled paper products where you can, or paper that is regulated and certified by an approved sustainable forest management and legal logging authority, such as the FSC (the Forest Stewardship Council) or PEFC (the Programme for the Endorsement of Forest Certification).

Grow your own

Getting involved with gardening and growing your own fruit and veg is rewarding in many ways. Not only is it good for the earth—as no packaging is required to get it to your table and there are no harmful chemicals involved—but it also allows you to spend time in the fresh air and experience the magic of bringing something to life!

- Start small—get a couple of pots, clear one small patch of your garden or have one raised bed to work with. As your confidence grows, so will your garden.

- If you're planting in the ground rather than in pots, understand what kind of soil you have, as this will affect how different plants grow.

- Install a water butt to collect rainwater. This means you have a completely free and eco-friendly source of water for your plants.

- Have a small supply of gardening tools to hand. The basics you'll need to get going are: plant pots and trays, a hand trowel, plant labels, a watering can and twine. Good-quality second-hand gardening equipment can be picked up very cheaply—and sometimes even for free. Before you buy anything new, look on the Freecycle website, where you should be able to find a dedicated Freecycle community in your area.

Research before you start planting. Make sure you're growing plants at the right time of year and in the right conditions.

Some good plants to start with if you are new to gardening are tomatoes, potatoes, radishes, zucchini or peas.

Try growing plants such as salad leaves and spinach. Not only are they easy to grow, but a little can be harvested every day and the leaves will keep on growing.

If you have a whole pack of seeds, plant them in batches so that they don't all mature at once.

Plant some flowers and herbs as well as vegetables. This will encourage pollinators to pay your garden a visit, so it will boost your crop.

Keep a record of your progress—where you plant things, which things grew well where, how the weather affected certain plants, and so on. This way, you can hone your gardening skills and strategy until it's just right.

Eco-friendly gardening

Here are ways to make sure your garden is green through and through:

- Select plants that are native. Non-native plants may wipe out native species, potentially unsettling the ecology of your garden and even the local area.

- If you're planting trees, choose varieties with large leaves and broad crowns, which are the most efficient at absorbing carbon and enabling photosynthesis.

- Grow succulents or alpines. They require significantly less fertilizer and, generally, less water than other kinds of plant.

- Avoid pesticides and opt instead for natural alternatives such as a mix of bicarbonate of soda and water to spray on fungal growth.

- Use recycled materials to grow and care for plants—from planting seeds in cardboard toilet rolls to covering a dormant veg patch with large flat pieces of cardboard to prevent weed growth.

🌿 Use "recycled" water in your garden—kitchen water and old bathwater (as long as you didn't use harmful soaps), or water from a water butt.

🌿 Avoid peat-based compost. Peat is mined from natural peat bogs, which destroys eco-systems and releases more carbon into the atmosphere. Opt for non-peat-based compost or make your own (see page 92).

🌿 Collect fallen leaves when they are wet, then store in trash bin bags for two years. The result is a nutritious leaf mulch which can be used to cover your most prized plants.

🌿 Old banana skins are rich in potassium and will do wonders for rose bushes when buried deep into the soil beside them.

🌿 To make a natural insecticide, mix 1½ tsp Castile soap with 1 liter (1.75 pt) water. Decant into a spray bottle and use as normal.

🌿 Use old CDs to deter birds from your precious crops. String up a few CDs with twine, shiny side out, and hang them from trees or garden canes.

🌿 Scatter some broken eggshells on your soil to deter slugs.

Composting tips

Composting is a great way to use up leftover food, plus it's a completely natural and free way to boost your garden. Here are some tips:

- Build your compost pile up from bare earth, beginning with a layer of twigs or straw a few inches deep.

- Have a container for kitchen waste and collect food scraps, peel, leftovers, teabags and coffee grounds. Take the container out to your compost bin when it gets full.

- If the aroma of leftover food is troublesome, keep food scraps in the freezer and empty out once a week for composting, or make sure that you have a container with a lid.

- Never put any meat, dairy, coal ash or excrement in your compost heap, as these will lead to unwanted pests and smells.

- Put in fallen leaves, plant and grass cuttings (as long as they don't have diseases), but avoid adding weeds.

- Include black and white newspaper or printer paper. Colored newspaper and magazines can also be composted so long as they're not covered in wax. Shred your paper before composting to speed up the process.

- Hair (yours or your pet's) is a great source of nitrogen for your compost!

- Fabric that is 100 percent cotton can be compostable—just remove all adornments and cut into strips. Synthetic fibers do not compost.

A sustainable wardrobe

The fashion industry is a big producer of waste, so we can do our part for the earth by being more mindful about our clothes. Here are some tips on having and wearing an eco-friendly wardrobe:

- Clothes are not supposed to be disposable. Cheap clothes that we wear a few times and get rid of might seem like a bargain, but they cost the earth. Change your mindset on clothes and think of them as an investment that will last.

- Buy from brands that care about the environment and produce their clothes sustainably. Carry out some research on your favorite stores to get a feel for their ethics.

- Look out for organic, fair trade fabrics or clothes that are made from recycled materials.

- Purchase pre-loved clothes. You could look in charity shops, or browse one of the many online sites that allow you to buy clothes second-hand. There are even sites where you can swap your clothes with other people.

Give the clothes that you no longer want to charity shops, clothing banks or friends and family, rather than throwing them away.

Repair your items when they break. Patch up holes, sew on new buttons or remove the lint from sweaters. All you need are some basic sewing skills, for which there are many online tutorials, or you can take your clothes to a local specialist.

Explore upcycling. If you have jeans with a rip, turn them into shorts. Cut up the material from a baggy sweater and make a hat. Turn an old dress into a blouse or top.

If your clothes have holes or stains and they're no longer good to wear, use them for cleaning, or repurpose the material.

When you feel the urge to buy something new for your wardrobe, consider whether you really need it. Will you use it often? Will it last?

Eco-friendly cosmetics

Our daily routines are often not very eco-friendly. Just to maintain a basic level of health and cleanliness, most of us use soap, shampoo, shower gel, scrubbers, toothpaste and toothbrushes, all of which involve lots of plastic and packaging. Here are a few ways to make your bathroom a more eco-friendly place:

- Use soap bars instead of liquid soap that comes with a plastic pump. If you enjoy crafting, you could even make your own. Tutorials for this can be found online.

- If you have to use plastic-pump soap, look for brands that allow you to buy refills rather than buying a whole new bottle each time.

- Instead of using disposable pads to remove make-up, make or buy reusable cotton pads that can be washed.

- Use a bamboo toothbrush instead of a plastic one. If you have an electric toothbrush, look for brands that allow you to return the heads to be recycled.

- Try toothpaste tabs rather than toothpaste— chew one of these small tablets to create your toothpaste rather than squeezing it out of a tube.

- Buy or make your own shampoo, conditioner and shower-gel bars, rather than relying on plastic-packaged liquid alternatives.

- Buy a single large tub of coconut oil for moisturizing, wiping away make-up, conditioning your hair and for use in homemade scrubs, rather than buying individually packaged items for each application.

- If you prefer to buy skin-care products such as moisturizer, look for refillable options.

- Use a natural loofah instead of one that is plastic-based.

- Invest in a metal razor rather than buying disposable plastic ones.

- Use cotton sanitary napkins that can be washed and reused, use a menstrual cup, or invest in specially designed period underwear that acts like a sanitary pad and can be reused.

- Choose stick deodorants instead of aerosols, to avoid the release of toxic chemicals into the environment.

- Look for toilet paper that's produced from recycled or sustainable sources.

Homemade beauty products

Being eco-friendly doesn't mean you can't pamper yourself from time to time. Here are a few simple beauty products you can make in your very own home, all with natural ingredients.

Exfoliating face scrub

Add 1 tbsp honey to 1 tbsp brown sugar (as fine as possible). With clean fingers, mix the two together, then apply to your face in small circular motions. Rinse with warm water.

Moisturizer

Combine ½ cup coconut oil with ½ tsp vitamin E oil and an essential oil of your choice. Mix thoroughly, then freeze for five to ten minutes. Using a fork, stir the mixture until it has a smooth consistency, and store in an airtight container. Apply as usual.

Soothing face mask

Mash one medium banana until smooth, and mix with ¼ cup plain yogurt and 2 tbsp honey.

Apply to your face and neck and leave for
10–20 minutes. Rinse off with cold water.

Foot soak

Fill a bowl or bath with 2 liters (3.5 pt) of warm
water. Add 35 g (1.25 oz) baking soda and
stir it in until it dissolves. Soak your feet for
30 minutes, then rinse them and pat dry.

Healthy hair mask

Mix 2 tbsp coconut oil, 4 tsp demerara (raw) sugar
and 3 drops peppermint essential oil. Apply the
mixture to clean, towel-dried hair that's still slightly
damp. Massage it into your scalp, then leave it
in for 10–20 minutes. Rinse with warm water.

Travel

Taking short journeys

If you're only taking a short journey, walk or cycle to your destination if you can. It's the most eco-friendly way to travel—plus it's good exercise and allows you to enjoy some time in the fresh air too! It's tempting to jump in the car to run small errands, but every little thing adds up, so try to walk wherever you can. The more you do it, the more it will become a habit.

An alternative for shorter journeys is taking the bus. Although there are some carbon emissions involved, it's far better for the environment than driving a car, and excellent if walking or cycling is difficult physically.

Taking longer journeys

For journeys that are too long to cycle or walk, buses, trains or coaches are all good options. The fact that each mode of transport carries tens or perhaps even hundreds of people on one journey lowers the overall carbon footprint of each passenger.

Flying

If you have to fly, try to choose an airline that has a smaller carbon footprint or one that offers carbon offsetting. Travel direct when you can—as take-off and landing are what use the most fuel—and choose economy class. Fly from your nearest airport to minimize the emissions caused by getting there, and travel as lightly as possible, because the lighter the plane, the less fuel is used! Flying will never be good for the earth, but if it's unavoidable, there are things you can to do make it more planet-friendly.

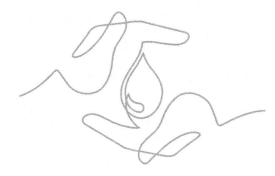

Making car travel greener

We can't escape the need to drive sometimes. Perhaps your destination is only reachable by car, or maybe you have to drive for your job. Don't worry! There are ways to make car journeys more eco-friendly. Take a look at the tips below.

- Check your car's tire pressures, as under-inflated tires can increase fuel consumption. You can usually find pumps at gas stations where you can read the current pressure for each tire and adjust it accordingly (consult your owner's manual for recommended pressures).

- Make sure that your car gets a regular service—a well-tuned car performs at an optimum level.

- Observe the speed limit and drive steadily without unnecessary stops and starts. This is the most efficient way to drive as it uses less fuel.

- If you're going to be stopped for more than ten seconds, turn the engine off as idling will waste more fuel.

Open the window rather than turning on the air conditioning.

Travel as lightly as possible, because the heavier the load, the more fuel your car will use. Remove roof racks or heavy items in your boot.

If you're buying a new car, consider a hybrid or electric model.

Lift-share with family, friends and colleagues. Whether you are giving the lifts or catching them with someone else, using one car to ferry multiple people to a destination is always better than using several!

Eco-friendly vacations

Can you travel while still looking out for the planet? The answer is yes! Here are some ways to minimize your impact on the world while you are exploring and experiencing it.

- Choose somewhere close to home as your destination to help minimize the emissions caused by travelling.

- If you do travel somewhere further afield, take a look at pages 100–103 on how to keep your carbon footprint low.

- Walking or camping vacations generally have a lower carbon footprint than city or beach breaks where you're using hotels, shops and restaurants.

- If you're staying in a hotel or hostel, look for one that's environmentally friendly. Is it energy efficient? Do they recycle? Do they have any environmental policies? Don't be afraid to get in touch to ask.

- Take a supply of reusable bags with you so that you don't need to buy any while you're away. It's also a good way to ensure that you

can take all your garbage home with you,
especially if you're walking or camping.

- Choose locally made food and drink
  products when you're shopping or eating at
  a restaurant. Not only does this support the
  local community, but these items are likely
  to have the lowest carbon footprints.

- If you're staying in a hotel, treat it as you would
  your own home. When you've paid for a room,
  there can be a temptation to "get the most out of
  it" by enjoying long, hot baths, having fresh towels
  every day and cranking up the air conditioning.
  However, although this might not cost you, it's the
  earth that has to pick up the tab—so keep this in
  mind next time you want to change your towel!

- If you're hiking, stick to the paths. Not only
  does this keep you safe, but it protects the local
  wildlife and ecosystems too and means you won't
  accidentally trample on endangered plants.

- Use public transport to travel around your
  destination rather than hiring a car.

- Look for eco-tourism vacations—these kinds of
  package vacations are specifically designed to
  support local communities financially and ensure
  that the tourism doesn't harm the environment.

Green gifts

Whether it's due to the colourful, glittery wrapping paper and ribbon, or the plastic packaging that they're presented in, gifts usually entail a lot of unnecessary waste. Here are some ideas about making Christmases, birthdays and any other gift-worthy celebration an eco-friendly event.

- Wrap gifts in brown paper as an eco-friendly alternative, and use natural twine if you want to decorate it. Or, even better: wrap up your gifts in cloth. In Japan, this practice is called *furoshiki*—look up tutorials online to learn how to execute beautiful and 100 percent eco-friendly gift-wrapping.

- Give experience gifts—there are so many different kinds available from pottery painting to stadium tours to Segway sessions. There are websites that cater specifically for this kind of gift.

- Give your time. Promise a friend a home-cooked meal, an afternoon's worth of gardening or an evening of babysitting. An extra thoughtful touch would be to create your own "voucher" so that your friend or family member can save the gift and choose when to use it.

🌿 Buy second-hand. There are plenty of incredible items to be found in charity shops and car boot sales. As they say, one person's trash is another person's treasure!

🌿 Donate some money on behalf of your gift recipient. You could plant a tree, sponsor an animal, buy chickens for a farmer or flowers for a care-home resident. Organizations such as goodgifts.org have plenty of options like this to suit any budget.

🌿 If you want to buy something new, try to buy from an eco-friendly company. Find out how they source their products and what their packaging is like.

🌿 If you're just sending a card, send an e-card to save on paper. You might think that e-cards lack the pizazz of the real thing, but there are all kinds that can come with songs and animations—have fun finding the perfect card for your recipient.

🌿 Why not create your own gifts? Whether you use your baking, crafting, DIY or upcycling skills, you'll be gifting something with a personal touch that's completely unique.

becoming
an
activist

Recycling in the home and using public transport is important, but the world needs to change if we're going to save it. So, become part of the solution! Everybody has a voice, and this chapter shows you how you can use yours to take action and enact change in your community.

Focus your energy

Saving the environment is a huge task, and there are so many ways to help out—so how do you know where to start? It's tempting to want to do everything you can to help, but in reality this will end up spreading you too thin. We all have limited time and resources, so pick one area to focus on and devote your energy to that. Perhaps there is a particular issue that you care about, such as animal welfare or preserving natural habitats. You could also be inspired by your local area; find out about the events that are happening, or initiatives that are being run and offer your support there. Whatever you do, remember that although we can't do everything, everybody can do *something*.

Start close to home

Think about the places in your own life where you could make positive changes. Could you campaign for your school to provide more recycling bins? At work, perhaps you could suggest ways to use less paper, push for more energy efficient lighting, or find an eco-friendly alternative to a coffee machine that uses plastic pods. To start making a difference, you don't have to look too far outside your own life. By talking to and inspiring the people around you, you will be able to work together to make lasting changes.

Join a group

Remember: you're not in this alone! There will probably be plenty of like-minded people around you who want to make a difference to planet Earth, and joining a group or club will connect you with them. You could join the local branch of a national eco-focused charity, or you could pick a cause that you care about—such as conservation or keeping beaches clean—and get involved that way. If you don't feel you can commit to joining a group, look out for volunteer opportunities where you can help out on the days that work for you. By working in a team, not only will you be able to help make the world a better place, but you'll be making new friends at the same time.

Demand change in your local area

To live in a truly eco-friendly world, changes need to be made by everyone, and campaigning in your local area is a good way to help kick-start this positive progress. Attend local government meetings to keep up to date with the issues that are being discussed, or apply to speak at one so that your concerns can be addressed. You could also speak one-on-one to your local representative—many will hold drop-in sessions where members of the public are free to come and discuss their ideas. Consider consultations too—these allow members of the public to have a say over upcoming policies, strategies and plans for the local area, so they are a good way to stay informed about your local government, and whether or not they have a green agenda.

Lobby your leaders

Lobbying the government means persuading politicians to support or speak out against certain policies or campaigns. For example, if you're aware that a new law is going to be passed that will have an adverse effect on the environment and you want to lobby for change, there are a number of actions you can take. You could write to or email your local government representative and ask them to vote against the law. You can often find email or letter templates online, but the most effective messages are ones written in your own words that include details about what the issue means to *you*.

Another option is to organize a petition, which you can do online. Try to create your petition through a government site if you can. If you're able to do this, it usually means that the petition has to be reviewed or debated once it reaches a certain number of signatures—making sure that the people in charge take notice of it.

Fundraise for relief efforts

Your energy and passion for the environment is a powerful tool—why not channel it into fundraising efforts? Money is often a big factor in whether or not environmental charities can continue their vital work, so raising funds on their behalf is a fantastic way to help out.

There are so many options for fundraising. Get together with a couple of friends and come up with a plan. If you want some inspiration about where to start, here are a few ideas:

- Have a fancy dress day at your school or work.

- Hold a charity auction.

- Organize a bake sale.

- If you're musical, play a gig with your band (even if it's just in your front garden!).

- If you're creative, make cards or small gifts and have a craft sale.

- Hold a bring-and-buy or rummage sale.

- Hold a charity sports game.

- Hold a trivia night.

- Have a sponsored silence.

- Hold a coffee morning.

- If you have a good team of people around you, try organizing a big event, such as a talent show, a sports day, a fair or a barn dance.

- Auction a special skill. Can you dance? Play an instrument? Speak another language? Offer to teach someone else what you know, and charge them a small fee for charity.

- Hold a karaoke night.

- Get sponsorship for completing a challenge— whether that's running a marathon, giving something up, wearing a crazy outfit for a day.

- Have a car wash for charity.

- Pack bags at a supermarket.

- Hold a raffle.

- Walk dogs around the neighborhood.

Take part in demonstrations

Show your commitment to the cause by taking part in a peaceful protest or a march. Look up whether there are any events happening in your local area, or whether there are any that you can travel to. Whether you're taking part in a small demonstration outside a local government building, or involved in a large march with thousands of other people, taking to the streets and standing up for what you believe in is a great way to support the climate change cause. Plus, it's empowering! Always bring plenty of water, some wet-weather protection (or hot-weather protection), a face mask and a fully charged phone, wear comfortable shoes as you might be standing up for a while—and don't forget a placard!

Be a keyboard warrior

You can be a climate-change activist even without leaving the house. Social media and the wealth of information online mean that there are plenty of things you can do to help the environmental cause with just your keyboard and an internet connection. Sign petitions and share them on your social media channels to give them a boost. Post news about climate change to raise awareness of the dangers we face, and share success stories to celebrate the milestones we reach along the way. Be vocal and show your support to companies who have eco-friendly policies—and get in touch with the ones who don't to ask them what they plan to do about it. Follow accounts that are dedicated to climate-change action to be inspired, and get involved in online communities who share your views. The digital world truly is your oyster!

Be creative

Making efforts every day to look after the environment can be hard work, especially when there seems to be more bad news than good. Keep the spark alive by being creative! Set yourself and your friends and family challenges that allow you to have fun while exploring planet-friendly lifestyle choices at the same time. How about having a produce-growing competition? Maybe you and a group of friends could upcycle something in your home rather than buying new. You could make some art for your home with only reclaimed products, have a plastic-free Christmas/birthday, or why not try a 30-day zero-waste challenge together with your household?

Find willing helpers

When you're fighting for the earth, you want as many people as possible to be on your side fighting with you. If you want to find new recruits, start by talking to the people who already want to do something rather than trying to convert people who oppose you. Keep your eyes out for people who have the same passion that you do; encourage them to be involved in your local groups, show them ways to live planet-friendly lives, and guide them toward resources to help them be the best climate-change advocates they can be. One day, they might be able to do the same for someone else.

What to say to skeptics

If you're vocal about climate change, going out into the world, marching, campaigning and acting, you're likely to encounter skeptics along the way, or people who just don't seem willing to talk about the environment. If you are in this situation, one of the most important things to remember is to stay calm. It can be disheartening and incredibly frustrating talking to people who don't want to confront the truth. However, if you want to connect with them and have any hope of changing their views, you need to approach your conversations with compassion.

Ask them about their views and find out what they think about the climate situation. Listen to what they say without interruption. Try to understand their perspective and what might have shaped their beliefs first, before jumping in to try to change their view. Rather than telling a skeptic they are wrong, offer them a counter-opinion. If you show that you are willing to listen to their side, they may be more willing to listen to yours. Remember to be gentle too: they might be experiencing eco-anxiety just like you—their skepticism may just be a different way of dealing with the feeling.

When talking to someone who is unconvinced about climate change, focus on the environmental effects that they might already be experiencing—such as weather extremes. To some people, climate change can seem like a distant thing that isn't affecting them, so using relatable examples connects them to the issue and brings it to life. For instance, someone may not care that much about wildfires and droughts on the other side of the world, but they will care about their own homes and families. This can be a way of establishing an emotional connection and common ground with someone else—which is a promising basis for discussion and understanding.

Last word

There's no escaping the fact that climate change is a threatening cloud on our horizon, so to be anxious for the future of the earth is a completely natural and justified reaction. However, eco-anxiety doesn't have to overwhelm us, and it is possible to be passionate about the planet without it being an all-consuming part of your life. By managing the fear that eco-anxiety brings us, by staying calm and optimistic, and by making planet-friendly choices every day, bit by bit we can help the earth and bring positive change to our own communities and the wider world.

There are also plenty of positives to take heart from! Take a look at the stories below to be inspired:

- The US and the European Union are increasing their use of renewable energy and, in 2019, the global carbon dioxide power sector emissions went down by 2 percent—this is the largest drop since records began in 1990.

- In 2019, wind and solar generated electricity rose by 15 percent globally, which means that it was responsible for 8 percent of the world's overall electricity use.

The southern jet stream is a wind that shapes weather patterns and ocean currents in the southern hemisphere. Since 2000, evidence showed that, due to ozone damage, its patterns were changing, causing catastrophic weather events in South America, Australia and East Africa. However, thanks to policies across the world putting regulations on ozone-depleting chemicals, the damage to the jet stream has started to be reversed.

More people are cycling than ever before. There has been an increase in the demand for bikes and e-bikes in the last few years and cities all over Europe are implementing more bike lanes; since May 2020, cars have been banned from the Rue de Rivoli in Paris, one of the busiest streets in the city.

There are many initiatives around the world focused on removing waste from rivers, marinas and oceans. One example is Dutch engineer Boyan Slat's solar-powered barge, *The Interceptor*, which can collect plastic from the ocean as it sails. At its best, it can collect 100,000 kg (220,000 lb) of litter per day!

As of February 2020, Luxembourg has made public transport free to the public to help encourage people to travel more sustainably.

There are huge reforestation projects set up all around the world. Not only will these projects restore damaged forests, but the increased number of trees also helps to remove harmful greenhouse gases from the air and improve air quality, regenerate soil for food and provide a habitat for a multitude of life forms.

In 2019, the United Kingdom established the Global Ocean Alliance, whose aim is to conserve 30 percent of the world's oceans by 2030. To date, over 22 countries have joined the alliance.

There are new strides being made in renewable energy research. Scientists are closer than ever to harnessing the power of artificial photosynthesis, which, if successful, could generate renewable energy from the carbon dioxide in our atmosphere.

We all have days when we feel hopeless or overwhelmed, so on these days look over the stories above and remember:

There is always hope to be found.

You are more powerful than you realize!

Every voice matters, and together we will make a difference.

Notes

....
....
....
....
....
....
....
....
....
....
....
....
....
....
....
....
....
....
....
....
....
....
....
....
....
....